CRITICAL THINKING
METHODS & CASES

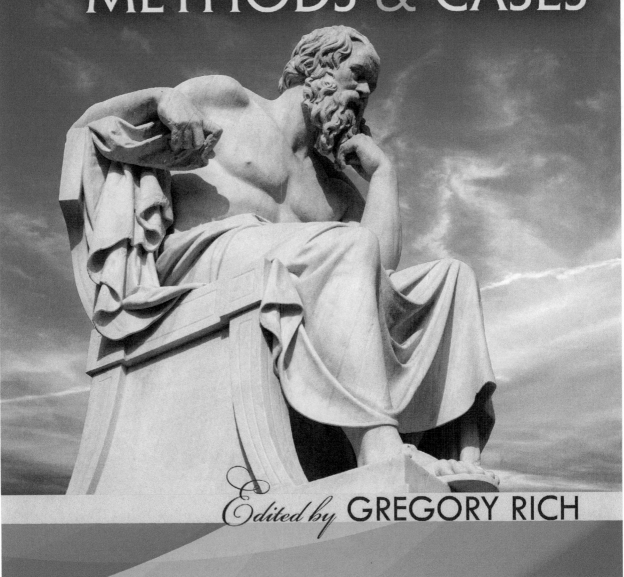

Edited by GREGORY RICH

Kendall Hunt
publishing company

Cover image © Shutterstock.com

KendallHunt
publishing company

www.kendallhunt.com
Send all inquiries to:
4050 Westmark Drive
Dubuque, IA 52004-1840

Copyright © 2017 by Fayetteville State University

ISBN: 978-1-5249-3731-7

Published in the United States of America

Table of Contents

Contributors

Ryan Beard, J.D. and Ed.D.

Paul Boaheng, Ph.D.

Wesley Dempster, Ph.D.

Marion Gillis-Olion, Ed.D.

Richard Hall, Ph.D.

Joseph Osei, Ph.D.

Gregory Rich, Ph.D.

"Hazing"

Developed by Gregory Rich, Marion Gillis-Olion, Joseph Osei, and Ryan Beard

© Slyvie Bouchard/Shutterstock.com

You will be preparing a written response to a hypothetical, but realistic situation presented in the following scenario. This assessment contains a series of documents that include a range of information sources. While your personal values and experiences are important, please answer all the questions solely on the basis of the information provided in the documents.

SCENARIO

As President of the Student Government Association (SGA) at Fine State University (FSU), you have called a special meeting of the SGA Executive Council to discuss some accusations about hazing on your campus. Ten other student leaders join you at the meeting. One of them, David Bowman, SGA Vice President, says that he has reason to believe that Tom Daniels, captain of the football team and president of Lambda Nu fraternity, is guilty of hazing some of his fellow students. David points to Documents A and B as evidence for his charge. Maintaining that hazing is wrong and citing Document C as support, he wants to report Tom to the campus authorities.

Tom is at this meeting as well. He says that there is no proof that he hazed anyone. He also says that even if he had done such a thing, there would not be anything wrong with it because plenty of campus groups engage in such practices as initiation rites, including the marching band, fraternities and sororities, and campus military groups. He concludes that even if there is compelling evidence that he did such things, he should not be reported, since there is nothing wrong in what he did. He cites Documents D–F in support of his views.

After a lively, extended discussion among the student leaders, you call for a vote. There is an even split among them on whether there is good evidence of hazing, on whether there is anything wrong with hazing, and on whether Tom should be reported. They ask you to cast the deciding ballot on all three matters. They also ask that you justify your decision in writing. They want you to use the information provided in Documents A–F to answer the following questions.

QUESTIONS

Now that you have read the scenario, answer the following three questions and justify your answers. Explain the reasons for your answers and justify those conclusions by referring to the specific documents, data, and statements on which your conclusions are based. Write in grammatically correct sentences that develop your points clearly and fully.

1. Is Tom guilty of hazing?

2. Is there anything wrong with hazing?

3. If there is good evidence against Tom, should he be reported to campus authorities for hazing?

In writing your justification, focus on the information presented in Documents A–F and consider the evidence on both sides of the question. Cite specific information in the documents to justify your position and reject the other position. For each question, support one position and criticize the opposing one. Name the documents as you consider them. Make it very clear why particular pieces of evidence in the documents are either good or flawed. Be sure to indicate very clearly which side you support in each case.

DOCUMENT A

An Excerpt from FSU's Policy on Hazing

"HAZING" Defined

The term "hazing" shall include, but not be limited to, pressuring or coercing a student into violating state or federal law; any brutality of a physical nature, such as striking in any manner, whipping, beating, branding, exposure to the elements, forced consumption of food, liquor, drugs, or other substances; or other forced physical activities that would adversely affect the health or safety of the student. It also includes any activity that would subject the student to extreme mental stress, such as sleep deprivation, forced exclusion from social contacts, forced conduct that would be extremely demeaning or results in extreme embarrassment, or any other forced activity that could adversely affect the mental health or dignity of the student. For purposes of this definition, hazing may occur whether the participation is voluntary or not voluntary.

DOCUMENT B

SGA Complaint Log

Date	Person Reporting	Report
9/12/13	Sarah Bellum	I was awakened at 3:00 AM last night, looked out the window, and saw a group of about five men chasing another group of five men as they turned the corner to go around the Butler Building heading toward the Chesnutt Library. They were all wearing dark T-shirts, so I recognized them right away as brothers and pledges of the Lambda Nu fraternity. I also recognized the president of that fraternity as one of the chasers; his baseball cap gave him away. The brothers in the fraternity must have been chasing after the pledges. It was clear to me that the brothers were trying to mistreat the pledges; otherwise, the pledges would not have been running from them.
8/23/13	Anonymous	I am writing to charge the captain of the FSU's football team with hazing the new members of the team. Yesterday, I saw him near the Student Center yelling at some of the new members of the team. I have also seen a video of him pushing around some of the team's new members. My suite mate heard a rumor that the captain is "very rough" and often threatens the new players with being cut from the team if they won't listen to him.

DOCUMENT C

Brochure from FSU's Counseling Office

"The Dangers of Hazing"

According to the *Concise Oxford English Dictionary*, to haze is "to torment or harass (a new student or recruit) by subjection to strenuous, humiliating, or dangerous tasks." Hazing violates FSU policy, and even those who voluntarily agree to undergo such treatment are being hazed.

Although hazing is against FSU policy and the law, it is still widespread. According to *Hazing in View: College Students at Risk,* a 2008 national study of student hazing, "55% of college students involved in clubs, teams, and organizations experience hazing" (2).

Widespread or not, hazing is dangerous. It can cause physical injuries, psychological problems, and even death. An *American Journal of Emergency Medicine* article, "Traumatic Injuries Caused by Hazing Practices," summarizes the potential injuries caused by various forms of hazing. It connects binge alcohol drinking to alcoholic coma and beating or striking to internal injuries. Michelle Finkel, MD, author of the article, says that hazing activities caused "at least 56 fraternity and sorority deaths from 1970 to 1999."

Student members of other kinds of organizations are also subject to hazing. According to *National Survey: Initiation Rites and Athletics for NCAA Sports Teams,* "one out of every five athletes (27 percent of men, 16 percent of women) participated in one or more *unacceptable* initiation rites, those that carry a high probability of danger or injury, or could result in criminal charges" (10). Marching band members also risk being hazed. The CNN website reports that in 2011, Robert Champion, drum major of Florida A & M University, died within an hour of being severely beaten by fellow band members (http://www.cnn.com/2012/05/14/us/florida-famu-hazing-death/index.html).

Hazing is too dangerous. Because it violates rights, it should not be practiced.

If you know of hazing on FSU's campus, please report it to this office or the Office of Student Affairs. That will show proper respect for your fellow students and help keep them healthy and safe. Show proper respect for yourself as well; don't allow yourself to be hazed. But if you know someone who is hazed, please help them seek medical attention right away in case they need it.

Candace Henderson, Head Counselor
FSU Counseling Office

DOCUMENT D

News Release with Blog

A New Study from State University Supports Hazing[*]

A University School of Psychology recently released a research study entitled "Hazing and Rites of Passage." The study concluded that media coverage of hazing deaths makes it too easy to think of hazing in a negative way, as something involving abuse, degradation, or law breaking. However, the paper provides evidence that most hazing and initiation practices have good results. They build the character of the newcomers and increase the unity of the organization as a whole. The author quotes an expert as saying, "The process, as bizarre and possibly degrading as it seems, does accomplish the desired goals of integration and socialization of new members and

---

[*]   http://www.stophazing.org/pro-hazing/pro-hazing-paper.pdf

solidarity of the group." The report also states that Japanese upper management trainees are subjected to boot camp–type experiences during training. Management consulting and training companies in America are also employing such "classes," where the emphasis is on working together as teams, overcoming harsh challenges, and building strong and confident leaders who appreciate their accomplishments.

BLOG COMMENTS:

Author	Topic: Why I Support Hazing
PM Charles	Posted May 10, 2012, 11:00 PM

"Hazing taught me how to persevere in the face of difficulties. By making me mentally and physically tough, it helped me prepare for the trials of life."

Kobe Wan	Posted April 14, 2012, 7:30 PM

"I agree. Even though swimming can be dangerous, that's not good reason to ban swimming. Similarly, even though hazing can be dangerous, that's not good reason to ban hazing. Sure problems may arise when hazers are angry or drunk, but most hazing is beneficial."

Fervently	Posted March 30, 2012, 11:40 AM

"Hazing is necessary for building the unity of a sports team or military unit. Those who don't think so are just weak or dumb."

DOCUMENT E

Letter from Lambda Nu Alumni Fraternity Brothers

Dear Lambda Nu President:

Recently, we have heard disturbing reports that some of the FSU administrators and younger brothers in your chapter of our Lambda Nu fraternity want to abolish our time-honored initiation rites. We are writing today to oppose this change.

First, we've always had these kinds of initiation rites; they're part of our tradition. They are part of what unifies us and makes us who we are, so they should not be abolished. Second, we had to go through theses rites ourselves, and they weren't always pleasant, to say the least. But if we had to go through them, so should those who want to become members today. Third, other fraternities have their own distinctive initiation rites, so why should we be any different? If everyone else does it, it should be ok.

Apparently, some of our younger brothers want to abolish the initiation rites because they believe the rites involve hazing. But these brothers fail to notice that no one is forced to go through these rites; it's all voluntary. Thus, since the pledges voluntarily choose to go through these rites, there's really no hazing involved.

Further, even if according to the school's policy, there is hazing, there's really nothing wrong with that. How can doing push-ups, shining shoes, wearing funny clothes around campus, or drinking a bit of alcohol do any harm?

You should also note that a recent research report cited on the "Greater Greek World" website shows that fraternities that have such initiation rites do more community service than fraternities that do not have such initiation rites.

Other younger brothers say that our fraternity must abide by the rules of the school and abolish the rites or risk being barred from campus. But we do not believe that continuing with the rites puts us at risk of being barred because plenty of faculty advisors and administrators already know about the rites and don't do anything about them.

Therefore, our fellow brother, we continue in our support of our traditional initiation rites, and we urge you to support them as well against those who aim to abolish them. Long live Lambda Nu! Long live our traditions!!

Sincerely yours,

Brothers Sam Dewey, Dave Cheetham, and Robert Howe, Attorneys at Law

DOCUMENT F

From the "Greater Greek World" Website

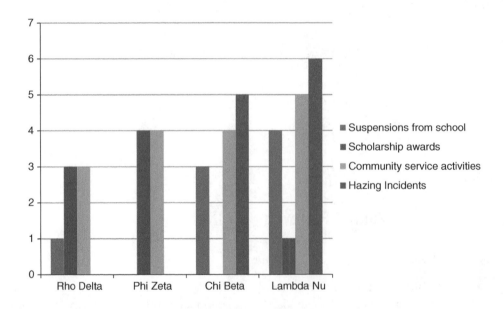

FSU's Office of Institutional Research provided the information in the preceding chart.

Covering the academic year of 2011–2012, this chart compares fraternities of equal numbers of members (20–25) that use traditional initiation rites with those that do not use them. Some people characterize those rites as involving hazing. Lambda Nu and Chi Beta use such rites, whereas Phi Zeta and Rho Delta do not.

As the chart shows, using such initiation rites *leads to* a greater involvement in community service activities. Such traditional initiation rites clearly have positive social consequences. Fears about traditional initiation rites are obviously exaggerated.

"Greater Greek World" website is sponsored and maintained by Dewey, Cheetham, and Howe Law Offices – "Go Greek."

QUESTIONS

1. What is the main claim that is being defended in the passage? It's the one for which evidence is being given.

2. What does the claim mean? Explain it in your own words.

3. In this passage, what evidence is offered for the main claim? The evidence is the ground or basis for believing that the main claim is true. Be sure to identify all of the evidence.

4. Is it reasonable to believe that the evidence is true?
   A. If so, why? For instance, is it from an unbiased credible expert on the topic in question? Or is it provided by a reliable eyewitness?
   B. If it's not reasonable to believe that the evidence is true, why not? For instance, are there other credible alternative explanations that have not been addressed or ruled out? Or is there strong evidence that the main claim is actually false?
   C. Be sure to assess all of the evidence and explain its strengths or weaknesses in detail.

4. Assuming that the evidence is true, would it show that the main claim must be true or that it is at least probably true? Be sure to check for fallacies in the reasoning.

5. Based on your analysis and evaluation, does the passage show that the main claim is true?
   A. If so, why?
   B. If the passage does not show that the main claim is true, then why not?

Critical Thinking and Writing

"Aggravated Assault Court Case"
Developed by Gregory Rich

© Antonio Guillem/Shutterstock.com

SCENARIO

On June 1, around 10:30 PM, Ms. Janet Burns, an 18-year-old black female, 5'3" tall and weighing 120 lbs, was stabbed with a knife in her lower back while she was using a pay phone near the street in front of the convenience store parking lot. Although seriously injured by the stabbing, she survived and recovered enough to return to her retail job in the mall.

Mr. Andre Swimmer, a 19-year-old black male, 5'7" tall and weighing 150 lb, was arrested for this crime and charged with aggravated assault.

The two main witnesses testifying against Mr. Swimmer are also African Americans. The first one is Mr. Alton Moore, the police officer who arrived on the scene soon after the stabbing. Based on evidence he collected at the scene, he arrested Mr. Swimmer within an hour of the stabbing. The second witness testifying against Mr. Swimmer is Mrs. Shante Green, a retired school teacher who claims to be an eyewitness to the crime.

QUESTIONS

You are on the jury that is hearing the case against Mr. Swimmer. As this is a criminal case, the judge has told you and the other members of the jury to presume the defendant, Mr. Swimmer, is innocent unless there is proof beyond a reasonable doubt of his guilt.

Your job is to determine whether the evidence given on the witness stand by Officer Moore and Mrs. Green is good enough to justify convicting Mr. Swimmer of aggravated assault.

Read Documents A–C. Then writing in sentences, answer the following questions:

Does the evidence given by Officer Moore and Mrs. Green show that Mr. Swimmer is guilty beyond a reasonable doubt? Why, or why not? Be specific and make sure that your answer comprehensively considers the evidence presented in the documents. Provide details from the documents to support your judgments.

DOCUMENT A

Legal Definitions

"Aggravated assault" =
"An assault where serious bodily injury is inflicted on the person assaulted … including assaults committed with dangerous or deadly weapons" (Gifis 33).

"Deadly weapon" =
"Any instrument that is capable of producing death or serious bodily injury … e.g., knife, pistol, rifle" (Gifis 126).

"Reasonable doubt" =
"Reasonable doubt which will justify acquittal is doubt based on reason and arising from evidence or lack of evidence, and it is doubt which a reasonable man or woman might entertain, and is not fanciful doubt … Reasonable doubt is such a doubt as would cause prudent men to hesitate before acting in matters of importance to themselves" (Black 1265).

Henry Campbell Black, et al., *Black's Law Dictionary*, 6th ed. (St. Paul, Minn.: West, 1990). Steven H. Gifis, *Law Dictionary* (New York: Barron's, 1996).

DOCUMENT B

Police Officer Alton Moore's Testimony on the Witness Stand

On June 1, when I arrived at the crime scene at 10:45 PM, I immediately went over to Ms. Janet Burns, an 18-year-old black female, approximately 120 lb and 5'3" tall, who was on a stretcher being lifted into an ambulance. She told me that she didn't know who had stabbed her, but that whoever had done it had snuck up behind her when she was using the pay phone in the convenience store parking lot and stabbed her in her lower back.

I then went over to the pay phone area, near the street in front of the convenience store, and put a crime scene tape around it to keep it from being disturbed. I couldn't inspect it thoroughly then because it was too dark for me to see the ground there since the streetlight right above it was burnt out and it was a dark night.

Then I walked 30 yards to the nearby convenience store. The clerk inside said she had been busy and had not seen anything of the stabbing.

Next I interviewed three young black males standing outside the store. The first one was Jerome Patterson, 19, 180 lb, and 6'2" tall. He was wearing black pants and a black t-shirt. The second one was Riley Brown, 21, 220 lb, and 6'4" tall. He was wearing an orange bathing suit and a white tank top. The third one was Anthony Watson, 20, 150 lb, and 5'8" tall. He had on blue jeans and a white t-shirt. He said that he was the victim's ex-boyfriend. All of these young men were very cooperative, and none said that he had seen anything of the stabbing.

Turning from them, I saw another young black male, Andre Swimmer, 19, 150 lb, and 5'7" tall, coming around the corner at the other end of the convenience store. He was wearing blue jeans and a white t-shirt. As I approached him to ask whether he had seen anything, he ran away from me. To me that was a sign that he was the guilty party.

After I caught up with him, I found even more evidence of his guilt. He was extremely nervous when I started asking him questions. I reasoned that if he was guilty, he would be very nervous when interviewed, and he was very nervous. So I concluded that he was the guilty party.

Plus when I searched him, he had a knife in his pocket that had some wet blood on its blade. He said that he had accidentally cut himself with the knife earlier in the evening when he was carving a walking cane, and so the blood on the knife was his. I asked to see the place he had cut himself, and he showed me a "cut place" on his finger. But I still found it hard to believe that the blood on the knife was his; he had such shifty eyes. He just acted and looked so guilty that I arrested him on the spot.

DOCUMENT C

Mrs. Shante Green's testimony on the witness stand

About 10:30 PM on June 1, I was sitting on my front porch on a hill that looks down at the convenience store parking lot. Even though I was about 100 yards from the convenience store parking lot, I saw Mr. Swimmer in the vacant lot beside the parking lot congregating with his friends, something they do there nearly every summer night.

I don't know what it is with these kids today. Their music is full of foul language, and they wear their pants down to their knees. They're lacking in good manners and good values. Mr. Swimmer, in particular, plays his boom box so loud in that vacant lot beside the convenience store that he often keeps me awake into the early morning hours.

That night I don't know what got into him, but I got a clear look at him stabbing that girl. I know it was night time, but I still have 20/20 vision even though I am 70 years old. It was easy for me to see him in his blue jeans and white t-shirt tiptoeing up behind the victim and then plunging the knife in her back. It's a wonder it didn't kill her.

Yes, I am positive that he's the one who did it. I saw it with my own eyes. The neighborhood needs to be protected from this dangerous young man, and so I hope he'll be locked up a long time for committing this crime.

QUESTIONS

1. What is the main claim that is being defended in the passage? It's the one for which evidence is being given.

2. What does the claim mean? Explain it in your own words.

3. In this passage, what evidence is offered for the main claim? The evidence is the ground or basis for believing that the main claim is true. Be sure to identify all of the evidence.

4. Is it reasonable to believe that the evidence is true?
    A. If so, why? For instance, is it from an unbiased credible expert on the topic in question? Or is it provided by a reliable eyewitness?
    B. If it's not reasonable to believe that the evidence is true, why not? For instance, are there other credible alternative explanations that have not been addressed or ruled out? Or is there strong evidence that the main claim is actually false?
    C. Be sure to assess all of the evidence and explain its strengths or weaknesses in detail.

4. Assuming that the evidence is true, would it show that the main claim must be true or that it is at least probably true? Be sure to check for fallacies in the reasoning.

5. Based on your analysis and evaluation, does the passage show that the main claim is true?
    A. If so, why?
    B. If the passage does not show that the main claim is true, then why not?

Critical Thinking and Writing

"Recycling"

Developed by Paul Boaheng

© Rawpixel.com/Shutterstock.com

SCENARIO

You are the president of the student government at Friendly State University (FSU). At the next student government meeting, the main question will be what needs to be done about recycling on FSU's campus. Some people favor hiring an external agency to be in charge of the school's recycling efforts. Others, however, want a campus group of volunteers, the Green Team, to continue leading the campus recycling efforts. You will need to listen to both sides and then make a recommendation to the chancellor.

Sateesh, a graduate student who has done numerous internships with environmental groups, proposes that the recycling efforts be turned over to a group called Sierra Recycling. He says Sierra Recycling comes to campuses across the country to help them start recycling programs at low cost.

Sateesh refers to **Document A** and argues: "It will be relatively inexpensive for Sierra Recycling to start a recycling program at our school." He maintains that other companies that provide the same services cost a lot more. Citing **Document B**, he further argues: "Universities that use Sierra Recycling have seen significant improvement in their graduation and retention rates; therefore, using the company will go a long way in improving FSU's graduation rate." Furthermore, citing **Document D**, Sateesh contends that the company that FSU Green Team sells the recycling to is under suspicion of collaborating with a company that is known to violate child labor laws in the production of its T-shirts and other clothing. Thus, FSU can salvage its reputation by hiring Sierra Company, a company that he believes is morally impeccable.

Another student, David, who is an ex-president of the student government at FSU, disagrees with Sateesh. David argues that since FSU already has an effective recycling program, it is economically imprudent to hire an external company to implement new recycling programs. He cites a letter, **Document C**, from Carolina Sustainability that praises FSU's current program. David refers to this document and argues: "FSU's recycling program is doing about as well as the campuses that have paid external agencies in charge of recycling. Thus, members of the Green Team should continue to educate students, staff, and faculty on recycling, reducing, and reusing materials to create an environmentally friendly campus community. They should continue to be in charge of FSU's recycling efforts." Lastly, David dismisses the moral charges against the company that FSU Green Team sells the recycling to as mere rumors, saying "I've never seen any solid proof of them. Even if the company is found guilty, it's not a big deal; since other campuses use that company, so why not FSU?"

QUESTIONS

As president of the student government, your role is to report to the chancellor of FSU on the strengths and weaknesses of the two contrary positions. You want to make the best recommendation, supported by credible evidence from the documents provided.

In answering the questions, explain the reasons for your conclusions, and justify those conclusions by explicitly referring to the specific documents and statements on which your conclusions are based. While your personal values and experiences are important, you should base your responses to the questions on the evidence provided in the documents.

1) Sateesh argues that other companies that provide the same services charge ridiculously high; therefore, FSU would save a lot of money by using Sierra Recycling Company. Sateesh further argues that universities that use Sierra Recycling have seen significant improvement in their graduation and retention rates and argues that using the company will help FSU improve its graduation rate as well. Using the documents provided, determine the strengths and/or limitations of his claims. Based on the evidence, what conclusion should be drawn about Sateesh's claims?

2) David argues that since FSU already has an effective recycling program, it is economically imprudent to invite an external company to implement new recycling programs. He advocates just sticking with the Green Team on Campus. Using the documents provided, determine the strengths and/or limitations of his claim. Based on the evidence, what conclusion should be drawn about David's claims?

DOCUMENT A

Costs of four companies

Year	Sierra Recycling	Cumberland Recycling	NC Recycling	SC Recycling
1	$75,000.00	$100,000.00	$150,000.00	$200,000.00
2	$150,000.00	$200,000.00	$300,000.00	$400,000.00
3	$300,000.00	$300,000.00	$450,000.00	$600,000.00
4	$600,000.00	$400,000.00	$600,000.00	$800,000.00
5	$2,000,000.00	$500,000.00	$750,000.00	$1,000,000.00

Source: FSU Office of Business.

DOCUMENT B

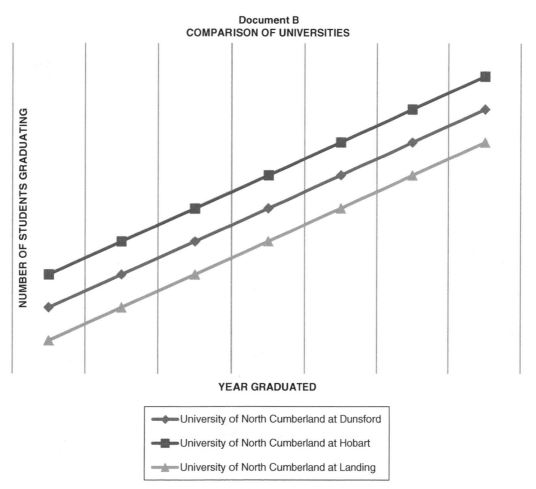

Document B
COMPARISON OF UNIVERSITIES

NUMBER OF STUDENTS GRADUATING

YEAR GRADUATED

- University of North Cumberland at Dunsford
- University of North Cumberland at Hobart
- University of North Cumberland at Landing

Source: University of North Cumberland Office of Internal Research

DOCUMENT C

A Letter from Carolina Sustainability—A Group of PhDs Specializing in Ecology

Dear FSU Student Body President:

Recently, you wrote our organization asking us to review the effectiveness of the Green Team's recycling efforts on your campus. You were particularly interested in knowing how your campus compares with other campuses that contract with external recycling agencies.

To answer your questions, I and a number of PhDs in Ecological Studies compared your school with three other comparably sized schools that use such for-hire agencies. I am happy to report that your school compares very favorably with these other schools. The table below summarizes our findings.

FSU, Comparably Sized Schools, and Their Recycling Programs, 2010–2011

	Mountain College—NC Recycling	FSU—Green Team	Western Maryland State College —Sierra Recycling	Suburban University— SC Recycling	Coastal Virginia University— Cumberland Recycling
Tons of recycled plastic	.52	.5	.51	.49	.48
Tons of recycled paper	8.1	8.77	7.5	8.6	8.43
Tons of recycled metal	5.11	5.13	4.98	5.0	6.0

Although you have a volunteer group, the Green Team, in charge of the recycling on your campus, you are doing about as well as comparably sized campuses that pay external agencies to lead recycling efforts.

Keep up the good work.

Sincerely yours,

James Brown, PhD
Executive Director of Carolina Sustainability

DOCUMENT D

A Letter Expressing Dissatisfaction with FSU Green Party

Dear Members of FSU Community:

I have been reliably informed that FSU is considering hiring Sierra Company to implement new recycling programs. I am writing to support this idea. Without a doubt, Sierra Company is one of the reputable companies in the world. The workers of the company, including my father, are so religious that they have never indulged in any immoral acts. Furthermore, the workers are highly competent religious leaders who are highly motivated to help students enjoy their studies. Indeed, a recent survey conducted by the General Secretary of Sierra Recycling Company has indicated that everyone is happy and satisfied with the services provided by Sierra Company.

By contrast, I have heard from many people that the company that FSU Green Party sells the recycling to is currently facing a cloud of moral suspicion. More specifically, the company is known to violate child labor laws in the production of its T-shirts and other clothing. While the company has not been found guilty yet, I think perception matters more than reality. Also, if the company is not really guilty, I don't think there will be all these rumors about the company. In every rumor, there is always a little bit of truth. As an alumnus of FSU, I am embarrassed that FSU would collaborate with such an immoral company. All my friends who graduated from FSU have expressed similar sentiments. Indeed, we have decided to withhold all our financial donations until FSU Green Party dissociates itself from this "immoral" company and hires Sierra Recycling Company to implement their new recycling programs.

Sincerely,

A Concerned Alumnus

QUESTIONS

1. What is the main claim that is being defended in the passage? It's the one for which evidence is being given.

2. What does the claim mean? Explain it in your own words.

3. In this passage, what evidence is offered for the main claim? The evidence is the ground or basis for believing that the main claim is true. Be sure to identify all of the evidence.

4. Is it reasonable to believe that the evidence is true?
   A. If so, why? For instance, is it from an unbiased credible expert on the topic in question? Or is it provided by a reliable eyewitness?
   B. If it's not reasonable to believe that the evidence is true, why not? For instance, are there other credible alternative explanations that have not been addressed or ruled out? Or is there strong evidence that the main claim is actually false?
   C. Be sure to assess all of the evidence and explain its strengths or weaknesses in detail.

4. Assuming that the evidence is true, would it show that the main claim must be true or that it is at least probably true? Be sure to check for fallacies in the reasoning.

5. Based on your analysis and evaluation, does the passage show that the main claim is true?
   A. If so, why?
   B. If the passage does not show that the main claim is true, then why not?

Critical Thinking and Writing

"Academic Integrity Violation"
Developed by Joseph Osei

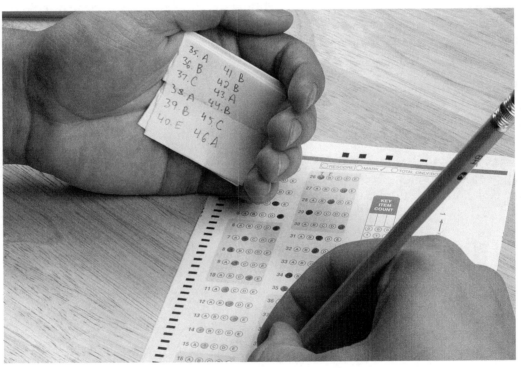

© Constantine Pankin/Shutterstock.com

SCENARIO

The *Friendly City Newspaper* has reported that two football coaches of Friendly City University (FCU) have been accused of illegally conspiring with some faculty for the last 20 years to secure passing grades for many of the school's student athletes. The coaches allegedly paid thousands of dollars to "friendly" faculty to sign up the students for Independent Study courses for which there were no meetings, syllabi, textbooks, or supervision. According to the Newspaper, the students in these courses have always been football players and have always been guaranteed a passing grade just for turning in a short essay on a topic of their choosing at the end of the term.

The Head of the Athletics Department, Mr. Adams, senses danger for the coaches and the faculty involved as well as for the reputation of the university. He's also concerned about the financial implications of such a scandal, so he calls an emergency meeting of the officers of the Student Government Association (SGA). Because you are the President of the SGA, Mr. Adams urges you and your fellow officers to organize a demonstration to deny the charges and show solidarity with the accused parties. Mr. Adams points out that this strategy of demonstrating has worked at least twice at other schools in the past 4 years.

Some of your fellow officers support Mr. Adams's point of view. Noting information in Document A, they maintain that the demonstrations are justifiable because there is nothing wrong with what the coaches, players, and faculty members have been doing. Referring to Document E, they also say that without the demonstrations, the school will most likely face a substantial financial loss as well as damage to its image. Other SGA officers, however, vehemently oppose the idea of demonstrating. Citing information from Documents B–D, they claim that there are strong moral objections to demonstrating in this case.

QUESTION

The meeting is now in a stalemate after 2 hours of debating the morality of such a demonstration. Since you are the President of SGA, your fellow officers ask you to resolve the dispute. They ask you to write a paper in which you review the evidence for both sides and then recommend either for organizing the demonstration or against it. Your **question** is

Is it morally right for the student leaders to organize a student demonstration to deny the charges and stand in solidarity with the accused coaches and faculty or not?

Prepare an argument in defense of your position with reference to the scenario and the attached Documents A–E. You should also explain why the other position is wrong and why the documents that seem to support it are not really good support for it. Write grammatically and clearly; develop your answers fully. Comprehensively consider the evidence. Name the documents and provide details from them to support your recommendation.

DOCUMENT A

"Is it ok for collegiate sports programs to cheat?"
Controversies in Sports Online Magazine
by Tod Man in Thoughts
October 23, 2016

According to conventional sports wisdom, there is no place for cheating in sports. After all, cheating is unfair. There are some, however, who say that they have to cheat because everybody else is doing it and it's the only way to be competitive. Is there something to be said for this last point of view?

Consider, for example, Florida State's perennial powerhouse football team. In 2006 and 2007, two tutors for at least 25 players on the team took quizzes for them and gave them answers for online tests. Did that help the student athletes do better on the field? No, the team had two of its worst seasons ever under its winning coach, Bobby Bowden: seven wins and six losses each season. Of course, that was before the cheating scandal became public, and then the National Collegiate Athletics Association (NCAA) punished the school by vacating five of its football victories in 2006 and all of its victories in 2007 (http://www.nytimes.com/2009/03/07/sports/ncaafootball/07ncaa.html).

Consider also, the case of the University of Minnesota basketball team. In 1999, just before an NCAA tournament game, an office manager for the team revealed that she had written term papers for a number of players on the team for the preceding 6 years. As a result, four players on the team were immediately suspended, and the team lost its tournament game. The team coach resigned once it became clear that he had been paying the office manager to write the papers. The NCAA sanctioned the school's basketball program by putting it on probation and reducing the number of scholarships it could offer (http://www.cbsnews.com/news/minnesota-put-on-4-year-probation/).

Would you agree then that such examples show that it's ok to cheat as long as others are cheating? A further question worth considering is "What if cheating leads to overall good consequences; will that make the cheating ok?"

DOCUMENT B

"Say *Yes!* To Friendly City University Football's Winning Tradition"

Hi Tony!

I've just received your email about your interest in signing up for the football team here at Friendly City University for your undergraduate degree. This is a no-brainer. There is no better place in the country for football student athletes than Friendly City University. You should have asked me a long time ago knowing that that's where I earned both my first degree and my MBA.

Friendly City University is not called friendly for nothing. All the coaches as well as the staff and the faculty are very friendly, especially toward football players, and will do all that they can to help you pass your courses and graduate with ease.

This is the way we do things here, the way we've always done them, and the way we'll continue to do them. This way was good enough for past generations at the school, and it's good enough for us as well. If you need a low grade to be changed to B or even A, just let the assistant coach know. Some of our professors have set up Independent Study courses just aimed at helping the football players out when they need a certain number of credit hours to graduate. I got two A's from two of such courses myself. Just give the instructor your name and student ID number and send him **any** essay – and I mean any essay – at the end of the term. The next day you'll see your grade on the computer; a smiling **B** or a flashy **A**. Voila!!

So let me know when you get to the campus. Just ask for the Business Office Manager in the Administration Block, and I'll introduce you to all these great people. Don't forget to bring some gifts from California for these new friends of yours. As they say, *"If you want a friend, be a friend."*

See yah!
Ben

DOCUMENT C

Extract from FCU's *Student-Athlete Handbook* on policies and procedures of the Athletic Department (loosely based on FSU's athletic handbook. Spring 2017) (http://grfx.cstv.com/photos/schools/fast/genrel/auto_pdf/2016-17/misc_non_event/Student-Handbook-2016.pdf)

I.   Our Philosophy

At FCU, we believe that true love and friendship are the keys to success in the classroom, on the athletic field, and in life beyond college. But love and friendship are not enough for success. So, we believe in complementing true love and friendship with honesty, integrity, respect for self and others, and, above all, good sportsmanship. Student athletes, as natural role models, must naturally obey all team rules, the National College and University Athletic Association (NCUAA) rules, as well as their college and university rules.

II.   Policy and Procedures on Academic Integrity

NCUAA defines academic dishonesty as the sharing, giving, taking, or presenting of information or material in any form by any medium with the intent of fraudulently or unethically helping oneself or another on any academic work, which is intended to be considered in the determination of a grade or the completion of academic requirements. Anyone who witnesses such a behavior has an obligation to report it immediately to the Dean of Students or his or her assistant. If you prefer to remain anonymous, your request will be respected without violation at any point.

III.   Academic Integrity Violations

A student shall be deemed guilty of the Academic Integrity Policy if he or she facilitates dishonesty by aiding another person to plagiarize, steal answers, or cheat on an academic assignment, including quizzes, take-home assignments, or tests. All student athletes should also remember that NCUAA prohibits any form of academic integrity violation, including paying someone or allowing a volunteer to complete their assignments or essays or tests on their behalf. It should also be noted that since FCU is a member of the NCUAA, any violation of NCUAA rules will be taken as violation of FCU rule.

IV.   Compliance Responsibilities

Student athletes have not only the obligation to avoid the violation of these laws but also the responsibility to report to the Athletic Director or the Dean of Students if they know or suspect any such violation of NCUAA rules, including violations by players, coaches, faculty, administrators, or members of the athletic staff.

V.   Possible Penalties for the School

The NCUAA reserves the right to suspend for a limited time or indefinitely any school which violates NCUAA rules. It can also ban permanently any school found guilty of egregious violations.

DOCUMENT D

Canvas Post from Ethics Teacher Regarding the Scandal

**E
T
H
I
C
S**

KEY

TO

THE

GOOD

LIFE

5 BASIC ETHICAL PRINCIPLES

1. DO NO HARM

2. BE HONEST

3. BE FAIR

4. RESPECT EVERYONE, INCLUDING YOURSELF

5. SHOW LOVE

The above are the 5 moral principles I was referring to in our conversation when you visited me last week. After all these years of teaching and coaching in middle schools, high schools and colleges, I still think they are the most basic moral principles everyone, students or faculty, should strive to live by, especially in academia.

REMEMBER: ALL THE PROPHETS AND PHILOSOPHERS AGREE THAT "A GOOD NAME IS BETTER THAN RICHES."

BUT DON'T FORGET: LOVE CONQUERS ALL.
Inspired by The Ethics Guy, Bruce Weinstein, PhD
Basic Ethics for Life.
www.The EthicsGuy.com

What is the most important thing about Ethics?
Don't leave home without it!

DOCUMENT E

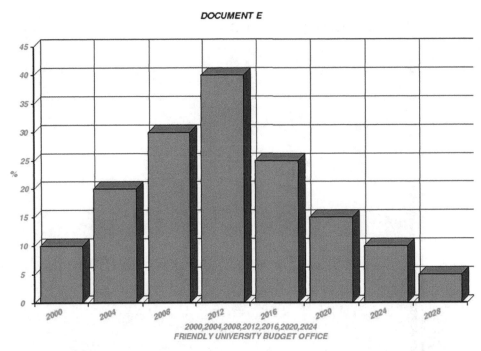

DOCUMENT E

2000,2004,2008,2012,2016,2020,2024
FRIENDLY UNIVERSITY BUDGET OFFICE

Record of financial benefits from FCU football game tickets 2000–2012 and estimated financial loss from 2012 to 2028. Should the football program be suspended?

QUESTIONS

1. What is the main claim that is being defended in the passage? It's the one for which evidence is being given.

2. What does the claim mean? Explain it in your own words.

3. In this passage, what evidence is offered for the main claim? The evidence is the ground or basis for believing that the main claim is true. Be sure to identify all of the evidence.

4. Is it reasonable to believe that the evidence is true?
    A. If so, why? For instance, is it from an unbiased credible expert on the topic in question? Or is it provided by a reliable eyewitness?
    B. If it's not reasonable to believe that the evidence is true, why not? For instance, are there other credible alternative explanations that have not been addressed or ruled out? Or is there strong evidence that the main claim is actually false?
    C. Be sure to assess all of the evidence and explain its strengths or weaknesses in detail.

4. Assuming that the evidence is true, would it show that the main claim must be true or that it is at least probably true? Be sure to check for fallacies in the reasoning.

5. Based on your analysis and evaluation, does the passage show that the main claim is true?
    A. If so, why?
    B. If the passage does not show that the main claim is true, then why not?

Critical Thinking and Writing

"Millsboro High School"

Developed by Gregory Rich, Wesley Dempster, Richard Hall, Joseph Osei, and Paul Boaheng

© Jannis Tobias Werner/Shutterstock.com

SCENARIO

School board officials in Millsboro, a small, rural, poor town in Morgan County, are concerned that public high school education in their town has become ineffective. The standardized test scores of their students do not compare favorably with those of other students in the state or with those in other states. To remedy the problem, the chairperson of the school board, Janice Green, proposes that a comprehensive tutoring program at the high school be instituted. In contrast, another member of the board, William Jones, wants to turn the high school over to a private contractor, College Bound, Inc.

To support his view, Mr. Jones puts forward two arguments. First, he says that Ms. Green's proposal to add a tutoring program will actually make the problem worse. His basis for this claim is a chart from a nearby school district showing a correlation between visits to the school's tutoring centers and low standardized test scores. This chart is Document A.

Mr. Jones also says that the money that would be used to establish the tutoring program could be better spent by bringing in College Bound, Inc., a private educational contractor, to run the school. To support this claim, he cites a newsletter from an educational society, the Avon Society, which endorses the program. The newsletter article is Document B. He also cites an educational research abstract in support of his position. It is in Document C.

QUESTION

Ms. Green hires you as a consultant to evaluate Mr. Jones's two arguments.

To do this, answer the following question: **Does Mr. Jones's evidence justify choosing the College Bound, Inc. program over the tutoring program?**

Be sure that you take a definite stand on the question and defend it with evidence from the documents. Consider the evidence on both sides of the question. Make sure that you evaluate the evidence in terms of whether it is good or bad. Cite specific information in the documents to support your position and reject the other position.

Your answers will be judged not only on the accuracy of the information you provide but also on how clearly the ideas are presented, how effectively the ideas are organized, and how thoroughly the information is covered.

DOCUMENT A

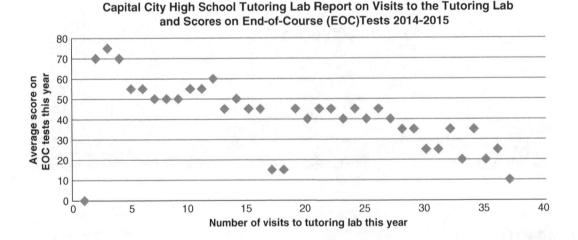

Capital City High School Tutoring Lab Report on Visits to the Tutoring Lab and Scores on End-of-Course (EOC) Tests 2014-2015

DOCUMENT B

Excerpt from *The Education Newsletter* – A Publication of the Avon Society[*]

"College Bound, Inc., Changes Education for the Better in Chicago"

To determine the worth of College Bound programs, consider the case of an inner-city high school in Chicago. Five years ago, the superintendent of schools there persuaded the school board to let College Bound run this new school. The superintendent made the right choice in turning the school over to College Bound, since there is strong evidence that College Bound is doing an excellent job.

Some of this evidence comes from the standardized test results of a group of students at the high school. These students completed algebra as freshmen, trigonometry as sophomores, and calculus as juniors. When these students took the Scholastic Achievement Test as sophomores, as juniors, and as seniors, their scores on the math part of the test showed steady, significant increases from 1 year to the next. Furthermore, in speaking of private education in general, basketball star LeBron James said last week, "Some private schools are better than many public schools."

From such evidence, it is clear that since College Bound works in this school, it should work in almost any other school. As a result, we at the Avon Society give the College Bound program our highest recommendation.

DOCUMENT C

Educational Abstracts: Educational Research and Outcomes Search

Search ID: far25quar/ddz.11
Search Date: October 17, 2016
Terms: Intervention Strategies for Low-Performing High Schools
1 Item Found

Author(s): Grant, J.
Locator: 2016, Rand, R. Tut. and Tech., 35-47

Abstract: A review was conducted of two types of intervention strategies used in 60 low-performing high schools. Whether these schools were located in rural, inner-city, or suburban areas, they all had low standardized test scores during the last 10 years. Thirty of the schools were turned over to three different private educational corporations (College Bound, Inc., Salamanca Educational Corp., and Educational Discipline), with each receiving 10 schools. The 30 remaining schools comprised a second group. These schools instituted new academic programs, including tutoring centers, peer mentoring, or multitrack course offerings. The majority of both groups of schools saw improvements in test scores over the first 3 years. Where there was improvement, the average degree of improvement was about the same for the private corporations as for the new programs. The degree of improvement varied considerably from school to school.

---

[*]   Avon Society is funded by DeVoss Enterprises, a group that advocates for private education.

QUESTIONS

1.   What is the main claim that is being defended in the passage? It's the one for which evidence is being given.

2.   What does the claim mean? Explain it in your own words.

3.   In this passage, what evidence is offered for the main claim? The evidence is the ground or basis for believing that the main claim is true. Be sure to identify all of the evidence.

4.   Is it reasonable to believe that the evidence is true?
    A.   If so, why? For instance, is it from an unbiased credible expert on the topic in question? Or is it provided by a reliable eyewitness?
    B.   If it's not reasonable to believe that the evidence is true, why not? For instance, are there other credible alternative explanations that have not been addressed or ruled out? Or is there strong evidence that the main claim is actually false?
    C.   Be sure to assess all of the evidence and explain its strengths or weaknesses in detail.

4.   Assuming that the evidence is true, would it show that the main claim must be true or that it is at least probably true? Be sure to check for fallacies in the reasoning.

5.   Based on your analysis and evaluation, does the passage show that the main claim is true?
    A.   If so, why?
    B.   If the passage does not show that the main claim is true, then why not?

Critical Thinking and Writing

"Creationism in Biology Classes"
Developed by Richard Hall

© Sergey Nivens/Shutterstock.com

SCENARIO

You are a member of a school board. A proposal has been made that intelligent design (creationism or creation science) should be taught in the public high school biology courses as a supplement to the theory of evolution by natural selection. Some have claimed that evolutionary theory is "only a theory" with serious flaws, among which it does not adequately explain the extraordinary complexity of such natural phenomena as blood clotting. You are responsible for making a recommendation to the board as to whether intelligent design should be part of the biology curriculum or not.

QUESTION

Should you recommend to the board that intelligent design be taught in public high school biology class to supplement the theory of evolution?

Be sure to make your recommendation clear and support it with evidence from the documents. Explain in detail why the evidence for your view is strong and the evidence for the other side has problems. Focus on the evidence in the documents and cover it comprehensively. Write clearly and grammatically.

REMEMBER

The issue is not whether evolutionary theory should be taught. It will be. The issue is whether it needs to be supplemented by the theory of intelligent design, which, its proponents claim, provides an adequate explanation of things that evolution by natural selection cannot.

DOCUMENT A

Definitions

"Evolution by Natural Selection":

Organisms inherit traits from their parents that enable them to adapt to their environments and so survive long enough to reproduce. Now if an offspring inherits a trait such as acuter vision or greater mobility enabling them to survive long enough to reproduce, then that trait will be passed on to the next generation of offspring and to generations thereafter. In the course of several generations, this adaptive trait spreads throughout the whole population of a species differentiating it from its ancestors to the degree that it becomes a new species.

From Lewis Vaughn, *The Power of Critical Thinking* (2nd ed.: New York: Oxford University Press, 2008), p. 398

"Intelligent Design":

According to the theory of intelligent design, such organs as the eye and the brain are far too complex to be explained adequately by the random and accidental processes supposed by natural selection. Such design in nature would have to be the result of the intentional creative efforts of an intelligent being, that is, God. To suppose that the eye or the brain is the result of the blind forces of nature is like supposing that a camera or computer simply happened by chance – and the design evident in the eye and brain is far more complex than that evident in these artifacts.

"Science":

Science is that system of knowledge beginning with observations, and then making inferences from them, and subsequently verifying or falsifying them through experiments.

DOCUMENT B

From Mr. Smith, a member of the school board above discussing the merits of creationism

Frankly, I am sick and tired of hearing about evolution, an adult fairy tale if there ever was one. Evolutionists are a pack of atheists who are not to be believed. The Holocaust happened because of Hitler's belief in evolution. Evolution can also be blamed for the rise in crime – if people are told that they are nothing more than evolved animals, they will act like animals. And, by the way, evolution is only a theory.

I would like to cite the opinion of U. S. Rep. Paul Broun on evolution as stated in the *LA Times* of October 7, 2012. His opinion should be taken seriously because he has had the honor of sitting in the House of Representatives. This is what he says:

"God's word is true. I've come to understand that. All that stuff I was taught about evolution, embryology, Big Bang theory, all that is lies straight from the pit of hell. It's lies to try to keep me and all the folks who are taught that from understanding that they need a savior. There's a lot of scientific data that I found out as a scientist that actually show that this is really a young Earth. I believe that the Earth is about 9,000 years old. I believe that it was created in six days as we know them. That's what the Bible says."

I too believe that the Bible is true because God wrote it. And I believe that God wrote it because the Bible says so.

DOCUMENT C

From Michael J. Behe, a professor of biochemistry at Lehigh University and a Leading Design Theorist

The sheer complexity of such things as the human eye, the mechanism whereby bacteria propel themselves, and the spontaneous clotting of blood surely could not have come about by accident.

Take the protein-induced clotting of blood as an example: If any of the many proteins that help clot blood were missing then blood could not clot. Such an all-or-none system could not have developed incrementally as supposed by evolution.

DOCUMENT D

From Mr. Jones, another member of the school board above discussing the merits of creationism

Balanced treatment for the competing biological theories sounds perfectly reasonable to me. After all, many reputable scientists support creationism, and the truth of evolutionary theory is very much in question. Having both sides presented should definitely increase student understanding of science.

Evolutionists often point to the existence of fossils in an attempt to support evolution over creationism. What they fail to realize, however, is that when God created the Earth less than 10,000 years ago, then for all we know, He could have also created the seemingly ancient fossils at the same time in order to test our faith. Since this is a biblically informed explanation of fossils, it is superior to the so-called "scientific" one based on evolution.

DOCUMENT E

Adapted from the National Academy of Sciences

Creationism conflicts with things we think we have very good reason to believe. Not only is there not scientifically credible evidence that the Earth is only a few thousand years old, but instead the overwhelming evidence, derived from the scientific method, is that the Earth is about 5 billion years old. In addition, evolution has much greater explanatory power than Creationism. For instance, evolution explains multiple diverse phenomena: (1) the emergence of new diseases; (2) the resistance of bacteria to antibiotics; (3) the molecular structure and dynamics of the cell; (4) the morphological similarities among different species. Evolution explains the facts of experience much better than Creationism. Further, as the distinguished geneticist Theodosius Dobzhansky has said, "Nothing in biology makes sense except in light of evolution." By contrast, Creationism does not make biology intelligible and fails to explain any of the above phenomena.

From Lewis Vaughn, *The Power of Critical Thinking* (4th ed.: New York: Oxford University Press, 2013), p. 399.

DOCUMENT F

From Mr. Evans, another member of the school board above discussing the merits of creationism

With all due respect, I cannot agree with Messrs Smith and Jones because I do not believe that creation science qualifies as a scientific theory at all. As such, then teaching it should not be mandatory for science classes. The way I see it, creation science is not a scientific theory because it relies on supernatural explanations, ones involving God. Such explanations, unlike scientific ones, do not lead to definite predictions about the natural world, and so do not provide a way for the theory to be tested. Scientific theories, however, are confirmed or disconfirmed through such tests and not by reliance on faith or the authority of a particular holy book. When scientists discuss changes in the weather, for example, they do not bring God into the picture at all. Instead, they rely on empirical observation and put the focus on the interactions among objects of nature. For this reason, then, I do not believe that the supernatural explanations of creation science belong in science classes.

Furthermore, this curricular decision appears to be one that should be decided by a consensus of scientific experts because they are the ones who know more about the subject. Though there are scientists who support giving equal time to creationism, they are a small minority. A large majority of scientists does not support equal time for creationism. In that case, giving equal time to creationism would create a false impression about the amount of disagreement there is in science about the credibility of evolutionary theory.

Being opposed to equal time for creationism in biology classes does not mean that one is anti-religious. For instance, unlike creationists, many Christians do not give a literal interpretation to the creation accounts in *Genesis*.

DOCUMENT G

A Poll Taken by Staff at the Creation Museum in Petersburg, Kentucky, on its Opening Day

A hundred patrons of the Creation Museum were interviewed on its day of opening. They all agreed that the museum made biblical truths come alive for them and clearly demonstrated the truth of creationism, based on the first two chapters of Genesis, and the falsity of evolutionary theory. According to one patron, Jim Bob Duggar, "We wanted to bring our family here to teach our children about creation and to show them all these great exhibits of how the world was created, and also to reinforce to them the fallacies of evolution and how it was impossible for this world just to all happen by chance."

QUESTIONS

1. What is the main claim that is being defended in the passage? It's the one for which evidence is being given.

2. What does the claim mean? Explain it in your own words.

3. In this passage, what evidence is offered for the main claim? The evidence is the ground or basis for believing that the main claim is true. Be sure to identify all of the evidence.

4. Is it reasonable to believe that the evidence is true?
    A. If so, why? For instance, is it from an unbiased credible expert on the topic in question? Or is it provided by a reliable eyewitness?
    B. If it's not reasonable to believe that the evidence is true, why not? For instance, are there other credible alternative explanations that have not been addressed or ruled out? Or is there strong evidence that the main claim is actually false?
    C. Be sure to assess all of the evidence and explain its strengths or weaknesses in detail.

4. Assuming that the evidence is true, would it show that the main claim must be true or that it is at least probably true? Be sure to check for fallacies in the reasoning.

5. Based on your analysis and evaluation, does the passage show that the main claim is true?
    A. If so, why?
    B. If the passage does not show that the main claim is true, then why not?

Critical Thinking and Writing

"Medicinal Water"

Developed by Gregory Rich

© marilyn barbone/Shutterstock.com

SCENARIO

You work in the marketing department of the Natural Remedies Company. Others working in the company contact you to propose new products for the company to market to the public. It is your job to determine whether their proposals are well supported by evidence. As part of your job, after you receive a proposal, you write a report to your supervisor in which you agree or disagree with the proposal. In the report, you explain the strengths or weaknesses of the evidence that has been provided to you.

Today, Gus Lands proposes that the company market bottled spring water from Russia as a pain reliever. His proposal reads as follows: "I've noticed that people will go to great lengths to live as pain free as possible. That's one reason I'm excited about a discovery I recently made in Russia. Folk healers there can "charge" water so that drinking it will significantly reduce pain. You're right to be skeptical about this "medicinal water," but after you review my attached evidence I believe you will agree with me. That evidence provides very good reason for Natural Remedies to market this water in the U.S."

QUESTION

Gus Lands puts forward Documents A–F as evidence for his proposal. Your question is **Does he offer good evidence for his proposal? Explain why or why not.**

Focusing on the evidence provided, explain and evaluate all of it. Give detailed support for your judgments, making specific references to the information presented in the documents. Explain fully, using your own words and writing in sentences.

DOCUMENT A

Testimony from the Folk Healers

According to the healers, the water works because they use their special power to charge it with an undetectable psychic energy. The healers point out that when most people drink the water for a few days after over-exercising, their muscle discomfort totally disappears. The healers credit the water for the reduction of the pain. They also say that, unlike most people, they can see a person's aura, a glowing light around the body, and then use that to tell the person's level of pain. Banking on their ability to see auras, they claim that those who drink the water have less pain than those who do not drink it. When asked how they can tell a person's level of pain just by looking at his/her aura, they say they just know because they have a special sense about such things.

DOCUMENT B

Survey at the Bottling Plant and the Wintergreen Center Study

A survey also supports the water's effectiveness. A random sample made up of 500 people working in the factories where the water is bottled and charged reveals almost unanimous agreement that the water is an effective pain reliever.

To seek further support for the survey results, the bottling company sent a team of its own investigators to observe arthritis sufferers who were participating in a 2-week Wintergreen Center retreat at a nearby beach. During the 2 weeks, the arthritis sufferers ate a special diet and engaged in regular daily exercise. The charged water was made easily accessible to them throughout their stay as well. At the end of the retreat, almost all of the arthritis sufferers reported that during the retreat, they had frequently drunk the water. Almost all of them also reported that their level of arthritic pain had gone down considerably from the beginning of the retreat to its end. Investigators maintained that the declines in pain were not at all likely to be coincidental, and perceiving no realistic competing explanation, they concluded that the charged water was the source of the declines.

DOCUMENT C

The Mountain–Desert Study

In this study, researchers compared a group of middle-aged adults from the mountains with a similarly constituted group of middle-aged adults from the desert, based on how much charged water they drank. The mountain group, unlike the desert group, drank plenty of the charged water. Researchers compared the degree of pain suffered by those who drank plenty of the water with the level of pain of those who did not. They found that 80% of those who drank plenty of the charged water said that their lives were generally free of aches and pain, whereas only 40% of those who did not drink the water said the same. Noting the correlation between drinking the water and living generally pain free, researchers claimed that drinking the water causes people to experience less pain.

DOCUMENT D

The Kazan experiment

Experiments also back up the water's effectiveness. In the Kazan experiment, investigators recruited a group of 20 headache sufferers. At 9 AM, the investigators gave the headache sufferers the charged water and told them that they were in an experiment to see whether the charged water would reduce their pain. At noon, investigators asked them about their pain level. Sixty percent of them reported a significant reduction in pain from their 9 AM level. This is conclusive confirmation that the water significantly reduces pain.

DOCUMENT E

The Moscow experiment

Other experiments also support the water's effectiveness. In a Moscow experiment, investigators divided a group of 200 headache sufferers in half. They gave one group charged water and the other group uncharged water as a placebo. The only other difference between the two groups was that the group getting the uncharged water included significantly more heavy alcohol drinkers and people with brain tumors. Investigators told each group that they were testing the effectiveness of the charged water. The results of this experiment were noteworthy. There were no differences between the two groups when they were asked whether the water relieved their pain. About one quarter of each group said that they felt better after drinking the water.

DOCUMENT F

The St. Petersburg Experiment

And finally, there is the St. Petersburg experiment. Investigators there divided a group of 300 headache sufferers in half, keeping the groups as much alike as possible. Again, one group got charged water and the other uncharged water as a placebo. In this case, the subjects did not know who was getting the charged water, but the investigators did. An investigator told the experimental group that he was sure they'd be feeling much better soon but made no such comment to the control group. Six out of ten in the experimental group but only two out of ten in the control group reported feeling much better after drinking the water they had been given. The investigators expressed satisfaction with the results, saying that they had been hoping for years to provide "scientific proof" of the water's effectiveness.

They remain confident about their results even though attempts on the part of other investigators in other labs have failed to replicate their "proof." The St. Petersburg investigators fully acknowledge that *many* other studies done on the charged water have not found any connection at all between consumption of the water and pain reduction. They say, however, that they are not bothered by this convergence of research against their point of view because those other investigators who came up with those results are skeptics and create such "bad vibes and negative energy" in the room that the water cannot work.

QUESTIONS

1. What is the main claim that is being defended in the passage? It's the one for which evidence is being given.

2. What does the claim mean? Explain it in your own words.

3. In this passage, what evidence is offered for the main claim? The evidence is the ground or basis for believing that the main claim is true. Be sure to identify all of the evidence.

4. Is it reasonable to believe that the evidence is true?
   A. If so, why? For instance, is it from an unbiased credible expert on the topic in question? Or is it provided by a reliable eyewitness?
   B. If it's not reasonable to believe that the evidence is true, why not? For instance, are there other credible alternative explanations that have not been addressed or ruled out? Or is there strong evidence that the main claim is actually false?
   C. Be sure to assess all of the evidence and explain its strengths or weaknesses in detail.

4. Assuming that the evidence is true, would it show that the main claim must be true or that it is at least probably true? Be sure to check for fallacies in the reasoning.

5. Based on your analysis and evaluation, does the passage show that the main claim is true?
   A. If so, why?
   B. If the passage does not show that the main claim is true, then why not?

Critical Thinking and Writing

"Who Shot Down Malaysian Flight MH17?"
Developed by Gregory Rich

© Keith Tarrier/Shutterstock.com

SCENARIO

On July 17, 2014, Malaysian flight MH17, which originated in Amsterdam, was flying over Ukraine bound for Kuala Lumpur. On the ground below, the Ukrainian army and Russian-supported rebels were fighting a war in eastern Ukraine. As MH17 passed over that area, it was shot down. All 298 occupants on this Boeing 777 civilian flight were killed. The immediate question was "Who shot down MH17?" The Ukrainians blamed the Russians, the Russian-backed rebels, or both. The Russians and the Russian-backed rebels both blamed the Ukrainians.

QUESTION

Suppose you are a researcher working for the International Court of Justice. In preparation for a possible trial regarding the downing of MH17, the legal team at the court asks you to review the evidence in Documents A–E to try to determine which side shot down the plane. There are basically two sides: (1) the Ukrainians did it or (2) the Russians, the Russian-backed rebels, or both working together did it. Your question is as follows.

Is the evidence that is provided good enough to determine which side shot down the plane?

Writing clearly and grammatically, take a definite stand on the question. Examine all of the evidence presented by both sides, weigh it, and see whether it better supports one side or the other. Cite details from the documents to support your judgments. Explain fully why evidence presented is strong or instead weak.

DOCUMENT A

Preliminary Findings of the Joint Investigation Team (JIT) on MH17 – from the British Broadcasting Company (BBC)

Soon after MH17 went down, the Dutch government organized the JIT, which included members from Holland, Belgium, Malaysia, Ukraine, and Australia. On September 28, 2016, the JIT gave a press conference and presented its preliminary findings on MH17.

According to the team, MH17 was shot down by a Russian-made Buk missile, which was fired from the rebel-controlled village of Pervomaiskyi (Pervomaiskoye), three miles south of Snizhne (Snezhnoye), in eastern Ukraine. Chief Dutch detective Wilbert Paulissen said that the missile and its launcher had come into Ukraine from Russia that day and returned to Russia the next day.

To support its claims, the JIT cited eyewitness testimony, played intercepted phone conversations, displayed photographs, revealed forensic evidence from the crash site, and referenced satellite imagery, among other things.

Ukrainian President Petro Poroshenko took the report as providing proof of blame. In contrast, Dmitry Peskov, press spokesman for Russian President Vladimir Putin, was not convinced that the report provided any proof at all (http://www.bbc.com/news/world-europe-37495067).

DOCUMENT B

Russian Military Officers, Engineers, and Media Present an Alternative

Soon after MH17 was shot down, high-level Russian military officers claimed that Russian radar had detected a Ukrainian SU-25 jet ascending quickly toward MH17. The officer noted as well that this jet, armed with missiles, could easily hit MH17 at that close range. He pointed to the jet as a blip on the radar screen after MH17 went down (https://www.rt.com/news/174412-malaysia-plane-russia-ukraine/).

Later in the year, the Russian Union of Engineers published a report in which they envisioned a jet using a combination of machine-gun fire along with missiles to bring down MH17 (https://www.newcoldwar.org/russian-union-of-engineers-point-to-ukraine-airforce-as-responsible-for-mh17-crash/).

They also put forward satellite imagery that they said showed a Ukrainian jet shooting down MH17. A Russian TV channel, Channel One, subsequently picked up this imagery and broadcast it as evidence that Ukraine was responsible for shooting down MH17 (http://tass.com/world/759835).

DOCUMENT C

Newspaper Article in the *Kiev Times*, "Was a Ukrainian Jet Responsible?"

Some Russian sources, including military officers and engineers, have advanced the theory that a Ukrainian SU-25 jet brought down Malaysian flight MH17. Their theory has many problems.

According to Nick de Larrinaga, an editor of *Jane's Defence Weekly*, a magazine focused on military and security options, including the capabilities of various weapons, the SU-25 with its nonpressurized cabin would not have been able to function well enough anywhere near MH17's high altitude (33,000 ft.) and so would not have been able to bring it down (http://www.bbc.com/news/magazine-35706048).

Also, the damage done to the flight deck area of MH17, as reconstructed from its wreckage, does not match the damage that would have been done had a SU-25 jet fired its heat-seeking missiles at the plane. Those missiles would have hit MH17's engines, its hottest parts. The main damage to MH17, however, was to its flight deck area. Experts agree that the best explanation of that damage involves a Buk missile explosion above the plane, which then propelled many pieces of shrapnel of different shapes into the plane (https://www.bellingcat.com/news/uk-and-europe/2015/01/10/su-25-mh17-and-the-problems-with-keeping-a-story-straight/).

In fact, one such piece of shrapnel was found embedded in the frame of the plane's front window (http://www.npr.org/sections/thetwo-way/2016/09/28/495747649/flight-mh17-was-shot-down-by-missile-moved-from-russia-investigators-say).

Finally, the satellite imagery that was broadcast on Russia's Channel One and purportedly showed a Ukrainian jet shooting down MH17 appears to have been a fake. As an article by Amy Knight in the *New York Review of Books* notes, the map images were put together from a variety of satellite maps, including Google maps, and the airline logo on the Boeing in the images does not match the logo on MH17 (http://www.nybooks.com/daily/2014/11/19/flight-mh-17-will-russia-get-away-it/).

DOCUMENT D

Russian Blogger Calls JIT Report Propaganda

The JIT report strongly suggests that Russians or Russian-supported separatists in eastern Ukraine used a Buk missile to shoot down Malaysian flight 17. Their report is pure propaganda; it's simply not true.

Eduard Basurin, a rebel military commander, pointed out that the rebels could not have done it, since they did not have any Buk missiles (http://www.bbc.com/news/world-europe-37495067).

Also, Major General Igor Konasjenko of the Russian Defense Ministry denied that any kind of Russian missile system had gone from Russia to eastern Ukraine. General Konasjenko proceeded to call into question the objectivity of the JIT report on the grounds that so much of it had come from the Internet and it was so heavily dependent on Ukrainian secret service sources (http://tass.com/politics/902838http://tass.com/politics/902838).

Russian Foreign Ministry spokesperson Maria Zakharova also branded the JIT investigation "biased and politically motivated." She said that the investigation unfairly favored Ukraine over Russia by giving Ukraine but not Russia a seat on the JIT. She said that, as a result, the Ukrainians could easily influence the course of the investigation in their favor. She claimed as well that the investigators arbitrarily sided with the Ukrainians and refused to give serious consideration to Russia's evidence about what really happened to MH17 (https://www.memri.org/reports/russia-week-september-28-october-5-2016).

Dmitry Peskov, President Putin's press spokesman, also raised a problem for the JIT report. He pointed to recently recovered Russian radar data that he said showed that any missile that shot down MH17 was not launched from eastern Ukraine, where the rebels were located (http://www.reuters.com/article/us-ukraine-crisis-mh-idUSKCN11Y0WN).

Other Russian sources, such as Almaz Antey, the company which manufactures the Buk, maintained that the missile was launched from a Ukrainian government-controlled area of Ukraine, and so the Ukrainians were the ones responsible for bringing down MH17 (http://www.telegraph.co.uk/news/2016/09/28/mh17-investigation-prosecutors-to-reveal-where-missile-that-down/).

Pavlov Ivanovich

½ Pravda Way

Moscow

DOCUMENT E

Dispatch from Associated Press Reporter Steven Dugan in Ukraine

The JIT did not arbitrarily reach its conclusions about the shooting down of MH17, as some high-level Russians have claimed. Around noon on July 17, 2014, I personally saw a Buk missile launcher in Snizhne (Snezhnoye), not far from Pervomaiskyi (Pervomaiskoye), where the missile was fired at MH17, according to JIT investigators. Many local people in the vicinity affirmed seeing the Buk as well (http://www.thedailybeast.com/how-we-know-russia-shot-down-mh17).

Intercepted phone calls between the separatist rebels and Russians provide reason to believe that the Buk came in that day from Russia. In the calls, a rebel leader requests a Buk to help protect his forces from Ukrainian air power, and later, he acknowledges receiving it (http://www.telegraph.co.uk/news/2016/09/28/mh17-investigation-prosecutors-to-reveal-where-missile-that-down/).

The Russians claim that the JIT was biased against them because it did not allow them full participation in the investigation. Investigators for the JIT claim that they did try to involve Russia in the investigation, even traveling there to request evidence. Even then, according to JIT investigator Paulissen, Russia did not provide documentary evidence even though repeatedly asked to do so (http://time.com/4512834/mh17-russia-buk-ukraine-evidence-putin/).

Two years after the JIT made its preliminary report, the Russians provided the JIT with the radar data that they claimed would show that the missile that brought down MH17 had not been fired from rebel territory (http://nltimes.nl/2017/05/16/russian-ukrainian-authorities-making-mh17-investigation-difficult-prosecutors).

The team, however, could not decipher the data, owing to its nonstandard format. As long as it is unreadable, it cannot prove that the rebels did not fire the missile. Far from being close-minded about the evidence, the JIT claims that it remains open to receiving further evidence from the Russians (https://www.flightglobal.com/news/articles/mh17-inquiry-grapples-with-russian-radar-data-format-434313/).

Perhaps the Russians' real worry is that the Ukrainians tampered with, or even fabricated, the JIT evidence. Yet, strangely enough, even rebel social media posts and Russian state media reports support the JIT findings. Right after MH17 was shot down, the rebels in the vicinity took to social media in an attempt to take credit for bringing down what they believed to be a Ukrainian cargo plane. Since no other plane was shot down in the area that day, they must have been referring instead to MH17. Until it was discovered that the plane shot down had been a civilian airliner, Russian state media repeated the rebels' claim about shooting down a Ukrainian cargo plane. One Russian state media source, Vzglyad.ru, even said that the separatists claimed that they had used a Buk missile to bring down the plane.

In the end, the JIT findings make better sense of the facts of the case than do the proposed Russian alternatives. For instance, Almay Antey, the Russian manufacturer of the Buk, claims that the Buk that brought down MH17 was fired from a Ukrainian government-controlled area. The separatists, however, claim to have controlled that area at that time (http://www.thedailybeast.com/how-we-know-russia-shot-down-mh17).

QUESTIONS

1.   What is the main claim that is being defended in the passage? It's the one for which evidence is being given.

2.   What does the claim mean? Explain it in your own words.

3.   In this passage, what evidence is offered for the main claim? The evidence is the ground or basis for believing that the main claim is true. Be sure to identify all of the evidence.

4.   Is it reasonable to believe that the evidence is true?
    A. If so, why? For instance, is it from an unbiased credible expert on the topic in question? Or is it provided by a reliable eyewitness?
    B. If it's not reasonable to believe that the evidence is true, why not? For instance, are there other credible alternative explanations that have not been addressed or ruled out? Or is there strong evidence that the main claim is actually false?
    C. Be sure to assess all of the evidence and explain its strengths or weaknesses in detail.

4.   Assuming that the evidence is true, would it show that the main claim must be true or that it is at least probably true? Be sure to check for fallacies in the reasoning.

5.   Based on your analysis and evaluation, does the passage show that the main claim is true?
    A. If so, why?
    B. If the passage does not show that the main claim is true, then why not?